JOHAN...
VO...

LETTERS FROM ITALY

TRANSLATED BY W. H. AUDEN
AND ELIZABETH MAYER

PENGUIN BOOKS

PENGUIN BOOKS

Published by the Penguin Group
Penguin Books Ltd, 27 Wrights Lane, London W8 5TZ, England
Penguin Books USA Inc., 375 Hudson Street, New York, New York 10014, USA
Penguin Books Australia Ltd, Ringwood, Victoria, Australia
Penguin Books Canada Ltd, 10 Alcorn Avenue, Toronto, Ontario, Canada M4V 3B2
Penguin Books (NZ) Ltd, 182–190 Wairau Road, Auckland 10, New Zealand

Penguin Books Ltd, Registered Offices: Harmondsworth, Middlesex, England

These selections are from *Italian Journey 1786–1788* by J. W. v. Goethe,
translated by W. H. Auden and Elizabeth Mayer, published by Pantheon Books.
This Penguin edition published by arrangement with Pantheon Books,
a Division of Random House, Inc.
This edition published 1995
1 3 5 7 9 10 8 6 4 2

Printed in England by Clays Ltd, St Ives plc

After fifty crowded lively hours I arrived here at eight o'clock last night, went early to bed and am now once more in a condition to continue with my narrative. On the evening of the ninth, after finishing the first instalment of my diary, I thought I would try to make a drawing of the inn, a post-house on the Brenner, but I was unsuccessful. I failed to catch the character of the place and returned indoors in somewhat of an ill-humour. The innkeeper asked me if I would not like to start on my way at once because the moon would soon be rising and the road was excellent. I knew that he wanted the horses back early next morning to bring in the second hay crop, so that this advice was not disinterested, but, since it corresponded with my heart's desire, I accepted it with alacrity. The sun came out again, the air was balmy: I packed and at seven o'clock I set off. The clouds had dispersed and the evening became very beautiful.

The postilion fell asleep and the horses trotted downhill at great speed along a road they knew. Whenever they came to a level stretch they slowed down. Then the driver would wake up and goad them on again. Very soon we came to the Adige, rushing along between high cliffs. The moon rose and lit up the gigantic masses of the mountains. Some watermills, standing above the foaming river among age-old pines, looked exactly like a painting by Everdingen.

When I reached Vipiteno at nine o'clock, it soon became obvious that they wanted me to leave at once. We reached Mezzaselva on the stroke of midnight. Everyone except the new postilion was fast asleep. On we went to Bressanone, where again I was, so to speak, abducted, so that I arrived in Colma as dawn was breaking. The postilions tore along the road so fast that it took my breath away, but in spite of my regret at travelling in such haste and by night through this lovely country, deep down inside I was happy that a propitious wind was behind me, hurrying me on towards my goal. At dawn I saw the first hillside vineyards. We met a woman selling pears and peaches.

On we drove. I reached Trinità at seven and was immediately carried off again. For a while we travelled north and at last I saw Bolzano, bathed in sunshine and surrounded by steep mountains which are cultivated up to a considerable height.

The valley is open to the south and sheltered on the north by the mountains of the Tirol. A balmy air pervaded the whole region. Here the Adige turns south again. The foothills are covered with vineyards. The vines are trained on long, low trellises and the purple grapes hang gracefully from the roof and ripen in the warmth of the soil so close beneath them. Even on the valley bottom, which is mostly meadowland, vines are grown on similar trellises, which are placed closely together in rows, between which maize is planted. This thrusts out higher and higher stalks: many I saw were ten feet high. The fibrous male flowers had not yet been cut off, for this is not done until some time after fertilization has taken place.

The sun was shining brightly when I arrived in Bolzano. I was glad to see the faces of so many merchants at once. They had an air about them of purpose and well-being. Women sat in the square, displaying their fruit in round, flat-bottomed baskets more than four feet in diameter. The peaches and pears were placed side by side to avoid bruising. I suddenly remembered a quatrain I had seen inscribed on the window of the inn at Regensburg:

> Comme les pêches et les melons
> Sont pour la bouche d'un baron,

Ainsi les verges et les bâtons
Sont pour les fous, dit Salomon.

Evidently this was written by a northern baron, but one can be equally sure that, if he had visited these parts, he would have changed his mind.

In the Bolzano market there is a lively traffic in silk; traders also bring cloth there and all the leather they can procure in the mountain districts. Many merchants, however, come mainly to collect money, take orders and give new credits. I should much have liked to inspect all the various products offered for sale, but my heart's desire will not let me rest, and I am as impatient as ever to leave at once.

I console myself with the thought that, in our statistically minded times, all this has probably already been printed in books which one can consult if need arise. At present I am preoccupied with sense-impressions to which no book or picture can do justice. The truth is that, in putting my powers of observation to the test, I have found a new interest in life. How far will my scientific and general knowledge take me? Can I learn to look at things with clear, fresh eyes? How much can I take in at a single glance? Can the grooves of old mental habits be effaced? This is what I am trying to discover. The fact that I have to look after myself keeps me mentally alert all the time and I find that I am developing a new elasticity of mind. I had become accustomed to only having to think, will, give orders and dictate, but now I have to occupy myself with the rate of exchange, changing money, paying bills, taking notes and writing with my own hand.

From Bolzano to Trento one travels for nine miles through a country which grows ever more fertile. Everything which, higher up in the mountains, must struggle to grow, flourishes here in vigour and health, the sun is bright and hot, and one can believe again in a God.

A poor woman hailed me and asked me to let her child ride in my coach because the hot ground was burning its feet. I performed this deed of charity as an act of homage to the powerful Light of Heaven. The child was dressed up in a peculiar and showy fashion, but I could not get a word out of it in any language.

The Adige now flows more gently and in many places forms broad islands of pebbles. Along the river banks and on the hills everything is planted so thickly that you would imagine each crop must choke the other—maize, mulberries, apples, pears, quinces and nuts.

Walls are covered with a luxuriant growth of dwarf-elder, and thick-stemmed ivy clambers and spreads itself over rocks; lizards dart in and out of crevices, and everything that wanders about reminds me of my favourite pictures. The women with their braided hair, the bare-chested men in light jackets, the magnificent oxen being driven home from the market, the little heavily laden donkeys—all this animated scene makes one think of some painting by Heinrich Roos.

As evening draws near, and in the still air a few clouds can be seen resting on the mountains, standing on the sky rather than drifting across it, or when, immediately after sunset, the loud shrill of crickets is heard, I feel at home in the world, neither a stranger nor an exile. I enjoy everything as if I had been born and bred here and had just returned from a whaling expedition to Greenland.

I even welcome the dust which now sometimes whirls about my coach, as it used to in my native land, and which I had not seen for so long. The bell-like tinkling noise the crickets make is delightful—penetrating but not harsh—and it sounds most amusing when some impish boys try to outwhistle a field of such singers: they seem to stimulate each other. Every evening is as perfectly calm as the day has been.

If someone who lives in the south or was born there were to overhear my enthusiasm at all this, he would think me very childish. But I already knew all about it when I was suffering, alas, under an unfriendly sky, and now I have the pleasure of feeling as an exception this happiness which by rights we ought to be able to enjoy as a rule of our nature.

TORBOLE, SEPTEMBER 12. AFTERNOON

How I wish my friends could be with me for a moment to enjoy the view which lies before me.

I could have been in Verona tonight, but I did not want to miss seeing Lake Garda and the magnificent natural scenery along its shores, and I have been amply rewarded for making this detour. After five, I started off from Rovereto up a side valley which discharges its waters into the Adige. At its head lies an enormous rocky ridge which one must cross before descending to the lake. I saw some limestone crags which would make fine subjects for pictorial studies. At the end of the descent one comes to a little village with a small harbour, or rather, landing place at the northern end of the lake. Its name is Torbole. On my way up the ridge I had frequently seen fig trees beside the road, and when I descended into the rocky amphitheatre I saw my first olive trees, which were laden with olives. I also saw, growing freely, the small white figs which Countess Lanthieri promised me.

From the room where I am sitting, a door opens on to the courtyard below. I placed my table in front of it and made a quick sketch of the view. Except for one corner to my left, I can see almost the entire length of the lake. Both shores, hemmed in by hills and mountains, glimmer with innumerable small villages.

After midnight the wind starts blowing from north to south. Anyone who wishes to travel down the lake must do so at this hour, for some hours before sunrise, the air current veers round into the opposite direction. Now it is afternoon and the wind is blowing strongly in my face, which is cooling and refreshing. Volkmann informs me that the lake was formerly called Benacus and quotes a line from Virgil where it is mentioned:

Fluctibus et fremitu assurgens Benace marino.

This is the first line of Latin verse the subject of which I have seen with my own eyes. Today when the wind is increasing in force and higher and higher waves are dashed against the landing place, the verse is as true as it was many centuries ago. So much has changed, but the wind still churns up the lake which a line of Virgil's has ennobled to this day.

In the cool of the evening I took a walk. Here I am really in a new country, a totally unfamiliar environment. The people lead the careless life of a fool's paradise. To begin with, the doors have no locks, though the innkeeper assures me that I would not have to worry if all my belongings were made of diamonds. Then the windows are closed with oil paper instead of glass. Finally, a highly necessary convenience is lacking, so that one is almost reduced to a state of nature. When I asked the servant for a certain place, he pointed down into the courtyard. *"Qui abasso può servirsi!" "Dove?"* I asked. *"Da per tutto, dove vuol!"* was his friendly answer. Everywhere one encounters the utmost unconcern, though there is noise and lively bustle enough. The women of the neighbourhood chatter and shout all day long, but at the same time they all have something to do or attend to. I have yet to see one idle woman.

The innkeeper announced with a true Italian flourish that he would have the happiness of serving me the most exquisite trout. These are caught near Torbole where a brook comes down from the mountains and the fish look for a way upstream. The Emperor receives ten thousand gulden for the fishing rights. They are a large fish—some of them weigh over fifty pounds—speckled all over from head to tail. They are not the real trout, but their taste is delicate and excellent—something between that of trout and salmon.

What I enjoy most of all is the fruit. The figs and pears are delicious, and no wonder, since they ripen in a region where lemon trees are growing.

SEPTEMBER 14

Now about my trip down the lake. This ended happily, after the beauty of the mirror-like water and the adjacent shore of Brescia had refreshed my whole being. Along the western shore, where the mountains were no longer precipitous and the land sloped more gently down to the lake, Gargnano, Bogliaco, Cecina, Toscolano, Maderno, Gardone and Salò stretched in one long row for about an hour and a half. No words can describe the charm of this densely populated countryside. At ten in the morning I landed in Bardòlino, loaded my baggage on to one mule and myself on to another. The road crossed a ridge which separates the lake basin from the Adige valley. The primeval waters from both sides probably met each other here, causing powerful currents which raised this gigantic dam of gravel. In quieter epochs fertile soil was then deposited on it, but the ploughmen are constantly bothered by the boulders which keep cropping up. They try to get rid of as many of them as possible by piling them on top of each other in rows, so that the road is lined by very thick and compact walls. Owing to the lack of moisture at this altitude, the mulberry trees are a sorry sight. There are no springs at all. Occasionally one comes across puddles of accumulated rain water, at which the mules and even the drivers quench their thirst. Below, along the river, water-wheels have been erected to irrigate the low-lying fields when necessary.

The magnificence of the new landscape which comes into view as one descends is indescribable. For miles in every direction, there stretches a level, well-ordered garden surrounded by high mountains and precipices. Shortly before one o'clock on September 14 I arrived in Verona, where I am writing this to complete the second instalment of my journal. Now I must sew the sheets together. I am greatly looking forward to seeing the amphitheatre tonight.

The amphitheatre is the first great monument of the ancient world I have seen, and how well preserved it is! When I entered it, and even more when I wandered about on its highest rim, I had the peculiar feeling that, grand as it was, I was looking at nothing. It ought not to be seen empty but packed with human beings, as it was recently in honour of Joseph I and Pius VI. The Emperor, who was certainly accustomed to crowds, is said to have been amazed. But only in ancient times, when a people were more of a people than today, can it have made its full effect. Such an amphitheatre, in fact, is properly designed to impress the people with itself, to make them feel at their best.

When something worth seeing is taking place on level ground and everybody crowds forward to look, those in the rear find various ways of raising themselves to see over the heads of those in front: some stand on benches, some roll up barrels, some bring carts on which they lay planks crosswise, some occupy a neighbouring hill. In this way in no time they form a crater. Should the spectacle be often repeated on the same spot, makeshift stands are put up for those who can pay, and the rest manage as best they can. To satisfy this universal need is the architect's task. By his art he creates as plain a crater as possible and the public itself supplies its decoration. Crowded together, its members are astonished at themselves. They are accustomed at other times to seeing each other running hither and thither in confusion, bustling about without order or discipline. Now this many-headed, many-minded, fickle, blundering monster suddenly sees itself united as one noble assembly, welded into one mass, a single body animated by a single spirit. The simplicity of the oval is felt by everyone to be the most pleasing shape to the eye, and each head serves as a measure for the tremendous scale of the whole. But when the building is empty, there is no standard by which to judge if it is great or small.

The Veronese are to be commended for the way in which they preserved this monument. The reddish marble of which it is built is liable to weather, so they keep restoring the steps as they erode, and almost all of them look brand-new. An inscription commemorates a certain Hieronymus Maurigenus and the incredible industry he devoted to this monument. Only a fragment of the outer wall is left standing and I doubt if it was ever even completed. The lower vaults which adjoin a large square called *il Bra* are rented to some artisans, and it is a cheerful sight to see these caverns again full of life.

The most beautiful of the city gates is called *Porta*

stupa or *del Palio*, but it has always been bricked up. From a distance it does not look well designed as a gate, and it is only when one gets close to it that one can recognize its beauty. All sorts of explanations are given for its being bricked up. Personally, I suspect that the artist intended it as a gateway to a new alignment of the Corso, for its relation to the present street is all wrong. To its left there are nothing but some barracks, and a line drawn at right angles to the gate through its centre leads to a nuns' convent, which it would certainly have been necessary to demolish. That was probably realized; also, the nobility and the men of wealth may have disliked the idea of building their houses in such a remote quarter of the town. Then, perhaps, the artist died, the gate was bricked up and the project abandoned for good.

SEPTEMBER 16

The portico of the Teatro Filarmonico looks very impressive with its six tall Ionic columns. By comparison, the life-size bust of the Marchese Maffei in an enormous wig, situated in a painted niche over the door, supported by two Corinthian columns, looks all the more puny. The place is honourable enough, but to be worthy of the grandeur of the columns, the bust should have been colossal. As it is, it stands ineffectually upon a little stone corbel and is out of harmony with the whole.

The gallery which runs around the vestibule is also too small, and the fluted Doric dwarfs look mean beside the smooth Ionic giants. But this must be forgiven for the sake of the fine museum which has been established under this colonnade. Here antique relics, most of them dug up in or around Verona, are arranged on exhibit. Some, even, are said to have been found in the amphitheatre. There are Etruscan, Greek and Roman works from the oldest times and some of more recent date. The bas-reliefs are set into the walls and bear the numbers Maffei gave them when he described them in his *Verona illustrata*. There are altars, fragments of columns and similar relics, also a beautiful tripod of white marble on which genii busy themselves with attributes of the gods. Raphael has copied and transfigured similar figures in the lunettes of the Farnesina.

The wind that blows from the tombs of the ancients is charged with fragrance as if it had passed over a hill of roses. The sepulchral monuments are intimate and moving and always represent scenes from everyday life. Here a husband and wife look out from a niche as from a window. Here a father and mother and son look at each other

15

with an indescribable tenderness. Here a married couple join hands, here a father reclines on a couch and appears to be chatting with his family. To me, the immediacy of these sculptures was extremely moving. They date from a late period in art, but all are very simple, natural and expressive. There is no knight in armour kneeling in anticipation of a joyful resurrection. With varying degrees of skill, the artist has represented only the simple realities of human beings, perpetuating their existence and giving them everlasting life. No one folds his hands or looks up to heaven. Here they are still the people they were on earth, standing together, taking an interest in each other, loving each other. All this, despite a certain lack of craftsmanship, is charmingly expressed in these works. A richly ornamented marble pillar also gave me something to think about.

Admirable though this museum may be, it is clear that the noble desire to preserve which inspired its founders is no longer alive. The precious tripod will soon be ruined, for it stands in the open and is exposed on the western side to the inclemencies of the weather. This treasure could easily be preserved by providing it with a wooden cover.

Had the Palazzo del Provveditore ever been finished, it might have made a fine piece of architecture. The nobility still build a good deal, but, unfortunately, everyone builds on the site of his old residence—often, therefore, in small, narrow lanes. At the moment, for instance, they are putting a magnificent façade on a seminary which is situated on an alley in one of the remotest suburbs.

As I was passing the huge, sombre gateway of a strange-looking building in the company of a chance acquaintance, he good-naturedly asked me if I would like to enter the inner courtyard for a moment. The building was the Palazzo della Ragione, and on account of its height, the courtyard seemed nothing more than an enormous well. "Here," he told me, "all criminals and suspects are held in custody." Looking about me, I saw that on every floor there was an open corridor railed off by iron bars, which ran past numerous doors. Whenever a prisoner steps out of his cell to be brought for interrogation, he gets a breath of fresh air but he is also exposed to the eyes of the public; since, moreover, there must be a number of rooms for interrogation, chains kept rattling in the corridors, now on this floor, now on that. It was a horrid experience and I must confess that the good humour with which I shook off the "Birds" would here have been put to a severer test.

At sunset I wandered along the rim of the crater-like amphitheatre, enjoying the view over the town and surrounding countryside. I was completely alone. Below me crowds of people were strolling about on the large flagstones of *il Bra*—men of all ranks and women of the middle class. From my bird's-eye view the women in their black outer garments looked like mummies.

The *zendale* and the *vesta* which constitute the whole *garderobe* of women of this class is a costume clearly suited to a people that does not care too much about cleanliness, but likes to move about in public all the time, now in church and now on the promenade. The *vesta* is a skirt of black taffeta worn over other skirts. If the woman has a clean white petticoat underneath, she knows how to lift the black one gracefully to one side. This is held in place by a belt which narrows the waistline and covers the lappets of the bodice, which may be of any colour. The *zendale* is a hooded shawl with long fringes; the hood is raised above the head on a wire frame and the fringes tied around the body like a scarf, so that their ends hang down at the back.

SEPTEMBER 17

I shall comment only briefly on all the pictures I have seen. My purpose in making this wonderful journey is not to delude myself but to discover myself in the objects I see. I must admit quite honestly that I understand very little about art or the craft of the artist, and must confine my observations to the subjects of the paintings and their general pictorial treatment.

The Church of San Giorgio is like an art gallery. All the pictures are altarpieces which vary in merit but all are well worth seeing. But what subjects these poor artists had to paint! And for what patrons! A rain of Manna, thirty feet long and twenty feet high, and, as a companion picture, the miracle of the Five Loaves! What is there worth painting about that? Hungry persons pounce upon some small crumbs, bread is handed out to countless others. The painters have racked their brains to give these trivialities some significance. Still, genius, stimulated by these demands, has created many beautiful works. One painter, faced with the problem of representing St. Ursula with her eleven thousand virgins, solved it very cleverly. The saint stands in the foreground, looking as though she has conquered the country. She has the noble, but quite unattractive, appearance of a virgin Amazon. In diminished perspective her little troop is seen stepping ashore from the ship and approaching in procession. Titian's Assumption of the Virgin in the Cathedral has become very black. One is grateful to this painter for letting the

Goddess-to-be look down at her friends below, instead of gazing up to Heaven.

In the Gherardini Gallery I found some beautiful things by Orbetto. This was the first time I had heard of him. When one lives far away, one hears only of the major artists in the galaxy and is often satisfied with merely knowing their names; but when one draws closer, the twinkle of stars of the second and third magnitude becomes visible until, finally, one sees the whole constellation—the world is wider and art richer than one had hitherto supposed. One picture I must especially praise. It contains only two half-length human figures. Samson has just fallen asleep in the lap of Delilah, who is reaching furtively across his body for a pair of scissors which lies on a table by a lamp. The execution is very fine. I was also struck by a *Danaë* in the Palazzo Canossa.

The Palazzo Bevilacqua houses many treasures. A so-called *Paradise* by Tintoretto—actually it is the Coronation of Mary in the presence of all the patriarchs, prophets, apostles, saints, angels, etc.—gave that happy genius the opportunity to display all his riches. To appreciate his vision, the facility of his brush and the variety of his expressive means, one would have to own this composition and have it before one's eyes for a whole lifetime. The technique is flawless. Even the heads of the most distant angels, vanishing into the clouds of glory, have individual features. The tallest figures are about a foot high; Mary and Christ, who is placing the crown on her head, measure about four inches. The loveliest creature in the picture, without any doubt, is Eve—still, as of old, a bit voluptuous.

A few portraits by Paul Veronese have increased my respect for this artist. The collection of antiques is magnificent, especially a son of Niobe prostrate in death. Most of the portrait busts, which include an Augustus wearing the civic crown and a Caligula, are interesting in spite of their restored noses. My natural disposition is to reverence the good and the beautiful, so, to be able to cultivate it day after day and hour after hour in the presence of such noble objects makes me feel very happy.

In a country where everyone enjoys the day but the evening even more, sunset is an important moment. All work stops; those who were strolling about return to their homes; the father wants to see the daughter back in the house—day has ended. We Cimmerians hardly know the real meaning of day. With our perpetual fogs and cloudy skies we do not care if it is day or night, since we are given so little time to take walks and enjoy ourselves out of doors. But here, when night falls, the day consisting of evening and morning is definitely over, twenty-four hours have been spent, and time begins afresh. The bells ring, the rosary is said, the maid enters the room with a lighted lamp and says: *"Felicissima notte!"* This period of time varies in length according to the season, and the people who live here are so full of vitality that this does not confuse them, because the pleasures of their existence are related, not to the precise hour, but to the time of day. If one were to force a German clock hand on them, they would be at a loss, for their own method of time measurement is closely bound up with their nature. An hour or an hour and a half before sunset, the nobility set out in their carriages; first they drive to the Bra, then down the long broad street to the Porta Nuova, through the gate and round the city walls. As soon as the hour of night rings, they all return; some drive to churches to recite the Ave Maria della Sera, others stop in the Bra, when the cavaliers approach the carriages and engage the ladies in conversation. This goes on for quite a while. I have never stayed to the end, but pedestrians remain in the streets until far into the night. Today it rained just enough to lay the dust. It was a gay and lively sight.

In order to adapt myself to one of the important customs of this country, I have invented a method which makes it easier for me to learn their system of counting the hours. The enclosed diagram will give you an idea of it. The inner circle shows our twenty-four hours from midnight to midnight, divided into two periods of twelve hours, as we count them and our clocks mark them. The middle circle shows how the bells are rung here at this time of year; they also ring up to twelve twice within twenty-four hours, but when our clocks would strike eight, they strike one, and so on till the twelve-hour cycle is completed. The outer circle shows how they reckon up to twenty-four. At night, for instance, if I hear seven strokes and I know that midnight is at five, I subtract five from seven and get the answer two in the morning. If, during the day, I hear seven rings and know that noon is at five, I do the same subtraction and the answer is two in the afternoon. But if I wish to refer to those hours according to local usage, I have to remember that noon is called seventeen hours; then I add this seventeen to the two and say nineteen hours. When you learn about this for the first time and start to figure it out, it seems extremely complicated and difficult to put into practice. But one soon gets used to it, and even finds the calculation as entertaining as the local inhabitants, who delight in this constant counting and recounting, like children who enjoy difficulties which are easy to master. They always have their fingers in the air, anyway, do all their counting in their heads and are fascinated by numbers.

Besides, the whole business is much easier for them because they do not pay the slightest attention to noon and midnight or compare, as we do, the two hands of a clock. They simply count the evening hours as they ring, and, during the day, add this number to the variable noon number with which they are familiar.

People here are always busily on the move, and certain streets where the shops and stalls of the artisans are crowded close together look especially merry. These shops have no front doors, but are open to the street, so that one can look straight into their interiors and watch everything that is going on—the tailors sewing, the cobblers stretching and hammering, all of them half out in the street. At night, when the lights are burning, it is a lively scene.

On market days the squares are piled high with garlic and onions and every sort of vegetable and fruit. The people shout, throw things, scuffle, laugh and sing all day long. The mild climate and cheap food make life easy for them. At night the singing and the music get even louder. The ballad of Marlborough can be heard in every street, and here and there a dulcimer or a violin as well. They whistle and imitate all kinds of birdcalls; one hears the most peculiar sounds. In the exuberance of their life this shadow of a nation still seems worthy of respect.

The squalor and lack of comfort in their houses, which shock us so much, spring from the same source; they are always out of doors and too carefree to think about anything. The lower classes take everything as it comes, even the middle classes live in a happy-go-lucky fashion, and the rich and the nobility shut themselves up in their houses, which are by no means as comfortable as a house in the north. They entertain company in public buildings. The porticos and courtyards are filthy with ordure and this is taken completely for granted. The people always feel that they come first. The rich may be rich and build their palaces, the nobility may govern, but as soon as one of them builds a courtyard or a portico, the people use it for their needs, and their most urgent need is to relieve themselves as soon as possible of what they have partaken of as often as possible. Any man who objects to this must not play the gentleman, which means, he must not behave as though part of his residence was public property; he shuts his door and that is accepted. In public buildings the people would never dream of giving up their rights and that is what, throughout Italy, foreigners complain of.

Today I strolled about the city studying costumes and manners, especially those of the middle classes, who are the most numerous and the most active. They swing their arms as they walk. Persons of higher rank, who wear swords on occasion, only swing the right arm, since they are accustomed to keeping their left arm at their side.

Though the people go about their business with such unconcern, they have a sharp eye for anything unusual. When I first arrived, everybody looked at my high boots, which, even in winter, are not worn here because they are too expensive. Now that I am wearing shoes and stockings, nobody any longer pays me attention. But early this morning, when they were all running this way and that with flowers, vegetables, garlic and other market products, to my great surprise they could not take their eyes off some cypress branches I had in my hands. These branches had green cones hanging from them, and I was also carrying some sprigs of blossom from a caper bush. Everybody, young and old, kept staring at my fingers, and strange thoughts seemed to be passing through their heads.

I had picked them in the Giardino Giusti, where huge cypresses soar into the air like awls. The yew trees, which, in our northern gardens, are clipped to a point, are probably imitations of this magnificent product of nature. A tree whose every branch, from the lowest to the highest, aspires to heaven and which may live three hundred years deserves to be venerated. Judging from the date when the garden was planted, these cypresses must already have reached such a great age.

VICENZA, SEPTEMBER 19

The road from Verona to Vicenza runs in a northwesterly direction parallel to the mountains. To the left one sees a continuous range of foothills, composed of sandstone, limestone, clay and marl, dotted with villages, castles and isolated houses. A vast plain stretches to the right, across which we drove on a wide, straight and well-kept road through fertile fields. There trees are planted in long rows upon which the vines are trained to their tops. Their gently swaying tendrils hung down under the weight of the grapes, which ripen early here. This is what a festoon ought to look like.

The road is much used and by every sort of person. I was delighted to see carts with low wheels shaped like plates and drawn by four oxen carrying large tubs in which the grapes are brought from the vineyards to the wine presses. When the tubs are empty, the drivers stand in them. It reminded me very much of a triumphal Bacchanalian procession. The soil between the vine rows is used for the cultivation of all kinds of grain, especially maize and mullet.

Near Vicenza a new range of hills rises, running north and south—they are said to be volcanic—which closes off the plain. At their feet, or rather in their semicircular recess, lies the city.

SEPTEMBER 19

I arrived some hours ago and have already seen the Teatro Olimpico and other buildings by Palladio. An excellent little book with copperplates and a text has been published for the benefit of foreigners by someone with an expert knowledge of art. You have to see these buildings with your own eyes to realize how good they are. No reproductions of Palladio's designs give an adequate idea of the harmony of their dimensions; they must be seen in their actual perspective.

Palladio was a great man, both in his conceptions and in his power of execution. His major problem was that which confronts all modern architects, namely, how to make proper use of columns in domestic architecture, since a combination of columns and walls must always be a contradiction. How hard he worked at that, how the tangible presence of his creations makes us forget that we are being hypnotized! There is something divine about his talent, something comparable to the power of a great poet who, out of the worlds of truth and falsehood, creates a third whose borrowed existence enchants us.

The Teatro Olimpico is a re-creation of a Classical theatre on a smaller scale and indescribably beautiful. Yet, compared to our own modern theatres, it looks like an aristocratic, rich and well-educated child as against a clever man of the world who, though not as rich, distinguished or educated, knows better what it is within his means to do.

Looking at the noble buildings created by Palladio in this city, and noting how badly they have been defaced already by the filthy habits of men, how most of his projects were far beyond the means of his patrons, how little these precious monuments, designed by a superior mind, are in accord with the life of the average man, one realizes that it is just the same with everything else. One gets small thanks from people when one tries to improve their moral values, to give them a higher conception of themselves and a sense of the truly noble. But if one flatters the "Birds" with lies, tells them fairy tales, caters daily to their weaknesses, then one is their man. That is why there is so much bad taste in our age. I do not say this to disparage my friends; I only say—that is what they are like, and one must not be surprised if things are as they are.

Beside the Basilica stands an old building resembling a citadel and studded with windows of unequal sizes. It is impossible to describe how wrong this looks. Undoubtedly the architect's original plan called for it to be demolished together with its tower. But I must control my feelings because here, as elsewhere, I so often come upon what I seek and what I shun side by side.

SEPTEMBER 21. EVENING

I called upon Scamozzi, an old architect who has brought out a book on Palladio and is himself a competent and dedicated artist. He showed great pleasure at my interest and gave me some information. The building of Palladio's for which I have a special predilection is said to be the house in which he himself lived. Seen at close range, there is far more to it than one would imagine from a picture. I should like to see a drawing of it in colour which would reproduce the tints that the stone and the passage of time gave it. But you must not think that the architect built himself a palace. It is the most unpretentious house in the world and has only two windows, separated by a wide expanse of wall which would easily have admitted of a third. One might make an amusing picture, showing how this house is wedged between its neighbours. Canaletto would have been the man to do this.

Today I went to see a magnificent house called the Rotonda. It stands on a gentle elevation half an hour out of town. It is a square block, enclosing a round hall lit from above. On each of the four sides a broad flight of steps leads up to a portico of six Corinthian columns. Architecture has never, perhaps, achieved a greater degree of luxury. Far more space has been lavished on the stairs and porticos than on the house itself, in order to give each side the impressive appearance of a temple. The house itself is a habitation rather than a home. The hall and the rooms are beautifully proportioned, but, as a summer residence, they would hardly satisfy the needs of a noble family. But from whatever direction one approaches it, the Rotonda is a fine sight. If one walks round it, the variety of visual effect created by the square block and the projecting columns is quite extraordinary. The owner's ambition, to leave his heirs an enormous *fidei-commissum* and a tangible memorial to his wealth, is perfectly realized. Just as the house can be seen in all its splendour from every point of the surrounding countryside, so the views of the countryside from the house are equally delightful. You see the

Bacchiglione gliding along as they steer their barges downstream from Verona to the Brenta, and you overlook the immense estates of the Marchese Capra, who desired that his family preserve them undivided. The inscriptions on the four gables, which together form a whole sentence, deserve to be recorded.

MARCUS CAPRA GABRIELIS FILIUS
QUI AEDES HAS
ARCTISSIMO PRIMOGENITURAE GRADUI SUBJECIT
UNA CUM OMNIBUS
CENSIBUS AGRIS VALLIBUS ET COLLIBUS
CITRA VIAM MAGNAM
MEMORIAE PERPETUAE MANDANS HAEC
DUM SUSTINET AC ABSTINET

The last line is very odd; a man who had so much wealth at his disposal and could do what he liked with it still feels that he ought to sustain and abstain. That lesson, surely, could have been learned at less expense.

I arrived here today, bag and baggage, after a three-and-a-half-hour drive from Vicenza in a single-seated little chaise called a *sediola*. The journey could have been made in half the time, but, as I wanted very much to enjoy a delightful day in the open air, I was not sorry that my *vetturino* failed to fulfil his obligation. We drove southeast across a fertile plain between hedges and trees without seeing anything special. At last, on the right, there rose a beautiful range of mountains stretching north and south. The profusion of flowers and fruits, hanging down from the trees and over the hedges and walls, was extraordinary. Roofs were laden with pumpkins, and the strangest-looking cucumbers hung from poles and trellises.

From the Observatory, I got a glorious view of the surrounding countryside. To the north lay the Tirolean Alps, snow capped and almost hidden in clouds, and joined in the northwest by the hills of Vicenza. In the west and nearer, I could make out distinctly the folded shapes of the hills of Este. To the southeast an unbroken plain stretched away like a green sea, tree after tree, bush after bush, plantation after plantation, and, peeping out of this green, innumerable white houses, villas and churches. The

Campanile of San Marco and other lesser towers of Venice were clearly visible on the horizon.

It was written, then, on my page in the Book of Fate that at five in the afternoon of the twenty-eighth day of September in the year 1786, I should see Venice for the first time as I entered the lagoons from the Brenta, and, soon afterwards, set foot in this beautiful island-city, this beaver-republic. So now, thank God, Venice is no longer a mere word to me, an empty name, a state of mind which has so often alarmed me who am the mortal enemy of mere words.

When the first gondola came alongside our boat—this they do to bring passengers who are in a hurry to Venice more quickly—I remembered from early childhood a toy to which I had not given a thought for perhaps twenty years. My father had brought back from his journey to Italy a beautiful model of a gondola; he was very fond of it and, as a special treat, he sometimes allowed me to play with it. When the gondolas appeared their shining steel-sheeted prows and black cages greeted me like old friends.

I have found comfortable lodgings in the Queen of England, not far from the Piazza San Marco. My windows look out on to a narrow canal between high houses; immediately below them is a single-span bridge, and opposite, a narrow, crowded passage. This is where I shall live until my parcel for Germany is ready and I have had my fill of sightseeing, which may be some time. At last I can really enjoy the solitude I have been longing for, because nowhere can one be more alone than in a large crowd through which one pushes one's way, a complete stranger. In all Venice there is probably only one person who knows me, and it is most unlikely that I shall meet him at once.

SEPTEMBER 29. MICHAELMAS EVE

So much has been said and written about Venice already that I do not want to describe it too minutely. I shall only give my immediate impression. What strikes me most is again the people in their sheer mass and instinctive existence.

This race did not seek refuge in these islands for fun, nor were those who joined later moved by chance; necessity taught them to find safety in the most unfavourable location. Later, however, this turned out to their greatest

35

advantage and made them wise at a time when the whole northern world still lay in darkness; their increasing population and wealth were a logical consequence. Houses were crowded closer and closer together, sand and swamp transformed into solid pavement. The houses grew upward like closely planted trees and were forced to make up in height for what they were denied in width. Avid for every inch of ground and cramped into a narrow space from the very beginning, they kept the alleys separating two rows of houses narrow, just wide enough to let people pass each other. The place of street and square and promenade was taken by water. In consequence, the Venetian was bound to develop into a new kind of creature, and that is why, too, Venice can only be compared to itself. The Canal Grande, winding snakelike through the town, is unlike any other street in the world, and no square can compete with the vast expanse of water in front of the Piazza San Marco, enclosed on one side by the semicircle of Venice itself. Across it to the left is the island of San Giorgio Maggiore, to the right the Giudecca with its canal, and still further to the right the Dogana with the entrance to the Canal Grande, where stand some great gleaming marble temples. These, in brief, are the chief objects which strike the eye when one leaves the Piazza San Marco between the two columns.

After dinner I hurried out without a guide and, after noting the four points of the compass, plunged into the labyrinth of this city, which is intersected everywhere by canals but joined together by bridges. The compactness of it all is unimaginable unless one has seen it. As a rule, one can measure the width of an alley with one's outstretched arms; in the narrowest, one even scrapes one's elbows if one holds them akimbo; occasionally there is a wider lane and even a little square every so often, but everything is relatively narrow.

I easily found the Canal Grande and its principal bridge, the Ponte Rialto, which is a single arch of white marble. Looking down, I saw the Canal teeming with gondolas and the barges which bring all necessities from the mainland and land at this point to unload. As today is the Feast of St. Michael, the scene was especially full of life.

The Canal Grande, which separates the two main islands of Venice, is only spanned by a single bridge, the Rialto, but it can be crossed in open boats at various points. Today I watched with delight as many well-dressed women in black veils were ferried across on their way to the Church of the Solemnized Archangel. I left the bridge and walked to one of the landing points to get a closer look at them as they left the ferry. There were some beautiful faces and figures among them.

When I felt tired, I left the narrow alleys and took my seat in a gondola. Wishing to enjoy the view from the opposite side, I passed the northern end of the Canal Grande, round the island of Santa Chiara, into the lagoons, then into the Giudecca Canal and continued as far as the Piazza San Marco. Reclining in my gondola, I suddenly felt myself, as every Venetian does, a Lord of the Adriatic. I thought with piety of my father, for nothing gave him greater pleasure than to talk of these things. It will be the same with me, I know. Everything around me is a worthy, stupendous monument, not to one ruler, but to a whole people. Their lagoons may be gradually silting up and unhealthy miasmas hovering over their marshes, their trade may be declining, their political power dwindling, but this republic will never become a whit less venerable in the eyes of one observer. Venice, like everything else which has a phenomenal existence, is subject to Time.

Towards evening I explored—again without a guide—the remoter quarters of the city. All the bridges are provided with stairs, so that gondolas and even larger boats can pass under their arches without difficulty. I tried to find my way in and out of the labyrinth by myself, asking nobody the way and taking my directions only from the points of the compass. It is possible to do this and I find my method of personal experience the best. I have been to the furthest edges of the inhabited area and studied the way of life, the morals and manners of the inhabitants. They are different in every district. Good heavens! what a poor good creature man is after all.

Many little houses rise directly from the canals, but here and there are well-paved footpaths on which one can stroll very pleasantly between water, churches and palaces. One agreeable walk is along the stone quay on the northern side. From it one can see the smaller islands, among them Murano, a Venice in miniature. The intervening lagoons are alive with innumerable gondolas.

Today I bought a map of the city. After studying it carefully, I climbed the Campanile of San Marco. It was nearly noon and the sun shone so brightly that I could recognize both close and distant places without a telescope. The lagoons are covered at high tide, and when I turned my eyes in the direction of the Lido, a narrow strip of land which shuts in the lagoons, I saw the sea for the first time. Some sails were visible on it, and in the lagoons themselves galleys and frigates were lying at anchor. These were to have joined Admiral Emo, who is fighting the Algerians, but unfavourable winds have detained them here. North and west, the hills of Padua and Vicenza and the Tirolean Alps made a beautiful frame to the whole picture.

OCTOBER 3

The Church of Il Redentore, another noble work by Palladio, has an even more admirable façade than that of San Giorgio. Palladio was strongly imbued with the spirit of the Ancients, and felt acutely the petty narrowmindedness of his times, like a great man who does not wish to conform to the world but to transform it in accordance with his own high ideals. From a casual remark in the book, I infer that he was dissatisfied with the custom of building Christian churches in the form of old basilicas, and tried to make his sacred buildings approximate to the form of the Classical temple. This attempt led to certain incongruities, which seem to me to have been happily avoided in Il Redentore, but are very conspicuous in San Giorgio. Volkmann says something about this but he fails to hit the nail on the head.

The interior of Il Redentore is as admirable as the exterior. Everything, including the altars, is by Palladio. Unfortunately, the niches, which were meant to be filled with statues, are occupied by mediocre figures, carved in wood and painted all over.

OCTOBER 5

This morning I visited the Arsenal, which I found most interesting because I am ignorant of naval matters and managed to learn a few elementary facts there. It was like visiting some old family which, though past its prime, still shows signs of life. I always enjoy watching men at work and I saw many noteworthy things. I climbed up on to a ship of eighty-four cannon, the finished hull of which was standing there. Six months ago, in the Riva degli Schiavoni, a similar ship burned down to the waterline. The powder magazine was not very full, so not much harm was done when it exploded; all that happened was that the houses in the neighbourhood lost their windows.

Watching the men working with the finest Istrian oak provoked some mental reflections on the growth of this valuable tree. I cannot repeat often enough how much my hard-won knowledge of those natural things, which man takes as his raw material and transforms to suit his needs, helps me to get a clearer idea of the craftsman's technique. Just as my knowledge of mountains and the minerals extracted from them is of great advantage to me in my study of architecture.

To describe the *Bucentaur* in one word, I shall call it a show-galley. The old *Bucentaur*, of which pictures still exist, justifies the epithet still more than the present one which, by its splendour, makes one forget the original. I always return to my old contention that any artist can create something genuine if he is given a genuine task. In this case, he was commissioned to construct a galley worthy of carrying the heads of the Republic on their most solemn day to the sacrament of their traditional sea power, and this task was admirably performed. One should not say that it is overladen with ornaments, for the whole ship is one single ornament. All the wood carving is gilded and serves no purpose except to be a true monstrance showing the people their masters in a splendid pageant. As we know, people who like to decorate their own hats like to see their superiors elegantly dressed as well. This state barge is a real family heirloom, which reminds us of what the Venetians once believed themselves to be, and were.

OCTOBER 7

For this evening I had made arrangements to hear the famous singing of the boatmen, who chant verses by Tasso and Ariosto to their own melodies. This performance has to be ordered in advance, for it is now rarely done and belongs, rather, to the half-forgotten legends of the past. The moon had risen when I took my seat in a gondola and the two singers, one in the prow, the other in the stern, began chanting verse after verse in turns. The melody, which we know from Rousseau, is something between chorale and recitative. It always moves at the same temp without any definite beat. The modulation is of the same character; the

43

singers change pitch according to the content of the verse in a kind of declamation.

I shall not go into the question of how the melody evolved. It is enough to say that it is ideal for someone idly singing to himself and adapting the tune to poems he knows by heart.

The singer sits on the shore of an island, on the bank of a canal or in a gondola, and sings at the top of his voice—the people here appreciate volume more than anything else. His aim is to make his voice carry as far as possible over the still mirror of water. Far away another singer hears it. He knows the melody and the words and answers with the next verse. The first singer answers again, and so on. Each is the echo of the other. They keep this up night after night without ever getting tired. If the listener has chosen the right spot, which is halfway between them, the further apart they are, the more enchanting the singing will sound.

To demonstrate this, my boatmen tied up the gondola on the shore of the Guidecca and walked along the canal in opposite directions. I walked back and forth, leaving the one, who was just about to sing, and walking towards the other, who had just stopped.

For the first time I felt the full effect of this singing. The sound of their voices far away was extraordinary, a lament without sadness, and I was moved to tears. I put this down to my mood at the moment, but my old manservant said: *"è singolare, come quel canto intenerisce, e molto più, quando è più ben cantato."* He wanted me to hear the women on the Lido, especially those from Malamocco and Pellestrina. They too, he told me, sing verses by Tasso to the same or a similar melody, and added: "It is their custom to sit on the seashore while their husbands are out sea-fishing, and sing these songs in penetrating tones until, from far out over the sea, their men reply, and in this way they converse with each other." Is this not a beautiful custom? I dare say that, to someone standing close by, the sound of such voices, competing with the thunder of the waves, might not be very agreeable. But the motive behind such singing is so human and genuine that it makes the mere notes of the melody, over which scholars have racked their brains in vain, come to life. It is the cry of some lonely human being sent out into the wide world till it reaches the ears of another lonely human being who is moved to answer it.

I visited the Palazzo Pisani Moretta to look at a painting by Paolo Veronese. The female members of the family of Darius are kneeling at the feet of Alexander and Hephaestus. The mother mistakes Hephaestus for the King, but he declines the honour and points to the right person. There is a legend connected with this picture according to which Veronese was for a long time an honoured guest in this palace and, to show his gratitude, painted it in secret, rolled it up and left it under his bed as a gift. It is certainly worthy of such an unusual history. His ability to create a harmony through a skilful distribution of light and shade and local colours without any single dominant tone is conspicuous in this painting, which is in a remarkable state of preservation and looks as fresh as if it had been painted yesterday. When a canvas of this kind has suffered any damage, our pleasure in it is spoiled without our knowing the reason.

Once it is understood that Veronese wanted to paint an episode of the sixteenth century, no one is going to criticize him for the costumes. The graded placing of the group, the mother in front, behind her the wife, and then the daughters in order, is natural and happy. The youngest princess, who kneels behind all the rest, is a pretty little mouse with a defiant expression. She looks as if she were not at all pleased at coming last.

My tendency to look at the world through the eyes of the painter whose pictures I have seen last has given me an odd idea. Since our eyes are educated from childhood on by the objects we see around us, a Venetian painter is bound to see the world as a brighter and gayer place than most people see it. We northerners who spend our lives in a drab and, because of the dirt and the dust, an uglier country where even reflected light is subdued, and who have, most of us, to live in cramped rooms—we cannot instinctively develop an eye which looks like such delight at the world.

As I glided over the lagoons in the brilliant sunshine and saw the gondoliers in their colourful costume, gracefully posed against the blue sky as they rowed with easy strokes across the light-green surface of the water, I felt I was looking at the latest and best painting of the Venetian school. The sunshine raised the local colours to a dazzling glare and even the parts in shadow were so tight that they could have served pretty well as sources of light. The same could be said of the reflections in the water. Everything was painted clearly on a clear background. It only needed the sparkle of a white-crested wave to put the dot on the *i*.

Both Titian and Veronese possessed this clarity to the highest degree, and when we do not find it in their works, this means that the picture has suffered damage or been retouched.

The cupolas, vaults and lateral wall-faces of the Basilica of San Marco are completely covered with mosaics of various colours on a common gold ground. Some are good, some are poor, depending upon the master who made the original cartoon. Everything depends on that, for it is possible to imitate with square little pieces of glass, though not very exactly, either the Good or the Bad.

The art of mosaic, which gave the Ancients their paved floors and the Christians the vaulted Heaven of their churches, has now been degraded to snuffboxes and bracelets. Out times are worse than we think.

The Casa Farsetti houses a collection of casts taken from the finest pieces of antique sculpture, a few of which I had already seen in Mannheim and elsewhere. A colossal Cleopatra with the asp coiled around her arm, sleeping the sleep of death—a Niobe shielding her youngest daughter from the arrows of Apollo with her cloak—a few gladiators—a winged genius resting—sitting or standing philosophers.

Many striking portrait busts evoked the glorious days

of antiquity. I feel myself, alas, far behind in my knowledge of this period, but at least I know the way. Palladio has opened it to me, and the way to all art and life as well. This may sound a little strange, but it is not quite so paradoxical as the case of Jacob Boehme, to whom Jove's thunderbolt revealed the secret of the universe while he was looking at a pewter bowl. The collection contains also a fragment of entablature from the temple of Antoninus and Faustina in Rome which, in its striking modernity, reminded me of the capital from the Parthenon which stands in Mannheim. How different all this is from our saints, squatting on their stone brackets and piled one above the other in the Gothic style of decoration, or our pillars which look like tobacco pipes, our spiky little towers and our cast-iron flowers. Thank God, I am done with all that junk for good and all.

Before the gate of the Arsenal, there are two enormous lions of white marble; one is sitting erect, planted firmly on his forepaws, the other is lying stretched out. They are so huge that they make everything around them look small, and one would feel crushed oneself if sublime works of art did not always elevate the spirit. They are said to belong to the best period of Greek art and to have been brought here from the Piraeus during the glorious days of the Republic.

Some bas-reliefs let into the wall of the Church of Santa Giustina, the vanquisher of the Turks, probably come from Athens as well, but they are difficult to see properly because of the high choir stalls. They show genii dragging about attributes of the gods. The sacristan drew my attention to them because, so the story goes, Titian took them as models for the angels in his painting; the Murder of St. Peter Martyr. They certainly are indescribably beautiful.

In the courtyard of a palazzo, I saw a colossal nude statue of Marcus Agrippa; the wriggling dolphin at his side indicates that he was a naval hero. How true it is that a heroic representation of the human being simply as he is makes him godlike.

I took a close look at the horses on the Basilica of San Marco. From below one can see that in some placed they have a beautiful yellow metallic sheen but in others show a copper-green tarnish. We are told that once they were gilded, and at close quarters one sees that they are scored all over, because the barbarians could not be bothered to file away the gold but hacked it off with chisels. Still, it might have been worse; at least their forms have been preserved.

Early this morning a gondola took me and my old factotum to the Lido. We went ashore and walked across the spit of land. I heard a loud noise; it was the sea, which presently came into view. The surf was breaking on the beach in high waves, although the water was receding, for it was noon, the hour of low tide. Now, at last, I have seen the sea with my own eyes and walked upon the beautiful threshing floor of the sand which it leaves behind when it ebbs. How I wished the children could have been with me! They would so have loved the shells. Like a child, I picked up a good many because I have a special use for them. There are plenty of cuttlefish about, and I need the shells to dry the inky fluid they eject.

Not far from the beach lies the Cemetery for the English and, a little further on, that for the Jews, neither of whom are allowed to rest in consecrated ground. I found the graves of the good consul Smith and his first wife. To him I owe my copy of Palladio, and I offered up a grateful prayer at his unconsecrated grave, which was half buried in the sand.

You must think of the Lido as a dune. The wind stirs up the sand, blows it in all directions and piles it up on all sides in drifts. Soon no one will be able to find this grave, though it is raised fairly high above the ground level.

What a magnificent sight the sea is! I shall try to go out in a boat with the fishermen; the gondolas dare not risk putting out to open sea.

Along the shore I found various plants whose common characteristics gave me a better understanding of their individual natures. All are plump and firm, juicy and tough, and it is clear that the salt content of the sand and, even more, the salt in the air is responsible. They are bursting with sap like aquatic plants, yet hardly like mountain flora. The tips of their leaves have a tendency to become prickly like thistles, and when this happens, the spikes grow very long and tough. I found a cluster of such leaves which I took to be our harmless coltsfoot, but it was armed with sharp weapons, and the leaves, the seed capsules and the stalks were as tough as leather. Actually, it was sea holly (*Eryngium maritimum*). I shall bring seeds and pressed leaves with me.

The fish market offers countless varieties of sea food. It is delightful to wander through it inspecting the luckless denizens of the sea which the nets have caught.

OCTOBER 9

A precious day from beginning to end! I visited Pellestrina, opposite Chioggia, where the Republic is constructing huge defences against the sea called *i murazzi*. These are built of uncemented stone blocks and are intended to protect the Lido in times of storm. The lagoons are a creation of nature. The interaction of tide and earth, followed by the gradual fall in level of the primeval ocean, formed an extensive tract of swampland at the extreme end of the Adriatic, which was covered at high tide but partly exposed at low.

Human skill took over the highest portions of ground and thus Venice came into being as a cluster of hundreds of islands surrounded by hundreds of other islands. At great cost and with incredible energy, deep channels were dredged to enable warships to reach the vital points even at low tide.

All that intelligence and hard work created in times past, intelligence and hard work have now to preserve. There are only two gaps in the Lido through which the sea can enter the lagoons—one near the Castello and one near Chioggia. Normally the tide flows in and out twice a day, and the current always follows the same course. The high tide covers the marshy patches but leaves the higher ground still visible, if not dry.

But it would be a very different matter if the sea should attack the spit of land and make new breaches so that it could flow in and out at will. Not only would the little towns on the Lido, Pellestrina, S. Pietro and others, be submerged, but also the system of communicating channels would be silted up. The Lido would be transformed into islands and the islands behind it into tongues of land. To prevent this, the Venetians must make every effort to protect the Lido, so that the angry element cannot destroy or alter that which man has already conquered and to which he has given shape and direction for his own purposes.

In times of abnormally high tides, it is especially fortunate that the sea can only enter at two points and is shut out elsewhere. The fury of its entry is curbed and in a few hours it has to submit again to the law of reflux.

Actually, the Venetians have little to worry about: the slowness with which the sea is receding guarantees them security for millennia, and, by intelligently improving their system of dredged channels, they will do their best to keep their possessions intact.

If only they would keep their city cleaner! It may be forbidden, under severe penalties, to empty garbage into the canals, but that does not prevent a sudden downpour from sweeping into them all the rubbish that has accumulated at the street corners, or, what is worse, from washing it into the drains, which are only meant to carry off water, and choking them, so that the main squares are in constant danger of being flooded. I have even seen the drains in the little square of San Marco, which are as sensibly distributed as those on the big one, choked to over-flowing.

On rainy days a disgusting sludge collects underfoot; the coats and *tabarros,* which are worn all year round, are bespattered whenever you cross a bridge, and, since every-body goes about in shoes and stockings—nobody wears boots—these get soiled, not with plain mud, but with a vile-smelling muck. Everybody curses and swears, but as soon as the weather clears up, nobody notices the dirt any more. It has been truly said that the public is for ever complaining that it is badly served but won't take the first step to see that it is served better. All this could be put right at once if the city authorities cared.

This evening I again climbed to the top of the Campanile. Last time I saw the lagoons in their glory at the hour of high tide; this time I wanted to see them in their humil-iation at low tide, so as to have a complete mental picture. It was very strange to see dry land all around where previously I had seen only a mirror of water. The islands were islands no longer but patches of higher ground rising from a large greenish-grey morass intersected by channels. The swampland is overgrown with aquatic plants and should, for that reason, be gradually rising, in spite of the pluck of the tides which never leave the vegetation alone.

To get back to the sea. Today I watched the amusing

behaviour of the mussels, limpets and crabs. What an amazing thing a living organism is! How adaptable! How there, and how itself! How useful my knowledge of natural history, scrappy though it is, has been to me, and how I look forward to increasing it! But, when there is so much to share with them, I must not excite my friends with exclamations alone.

The sea walls of which I spoke are constructed as follows. First come some steep steps, then a gently inclined surface, then another step, then another incline and finally a vertical wall with a coping on top. The rising sea climbs the steps and slopes and only when exceptionally violent does it break against the wall and its coping.

In the wake of the tide come small mussels, univalved limpets and any other small creature that is capable of motion, crabs in particular. But they have hardly secured a hold on the sea wall before the tide begins to recede. At first the crawling swarm does not know what has happened to it, and expects the briny flood to return. But it does not return. The stone quickly dries in the blazing sun, and, at that, they begin to beat a hasty retreat. This gives the crabs their chance to go hunting. Nothing is more entertaining to watch than the movements of these creatures. All one can see is a round body and two long pincer claws; their spindly legs are invisible. They strut along as if on stilts, and as soon as a limpet starts moving, they rush forward and try to insert their claws into the narrow span between the limpet's shell and the ground so as to turn it upside down and devour the now defenceless mollusc. But as soon as the limpet senses the presence of its enemy, it attaches itself to the stone by suction. Now the crab puts on a bizarre and graceful performance. It capers around the shell like a monkey, but lacks the strength to overpower the powerful muscle of the soft little creature. Presently it abandons its quarry and hurries off to stalk another wanderer, while the first limpet continues slowly on its way. I did not see a single crab succeed, although I watched for hours.

OCTOBER 12

Having gone over my journal for the last time and inserted a few observations from my notes, I shall now arrange everything in the proper order, roll it up and send it off, to be submitted to the judgment of my friends.

There is much in this record, I know, which I could have described more accurately, amplified and improved, but I shall leave everything as it stands because first impressions, even if they are not always correct, are valuable and precious to us. Oh, if only I could end my distant friends a breath of the more carefree existence here! It is true that the Italian has only the shadowiest idea of the ultramontane countries, but Beyond the Alps now seems dim to me too, though friendly faces beckon to me all the time out of the mists. The climate alone would lead me to prefer these regions to all others, if birth and habit were not powerful bonds. I should not like to live here permanently or anywhere else where I had no occupation. For the present the novelty of everything keeps me constantly busy. Architecture rises out of its grave like a ghost from the past, and exhorts me to study its precepts, not in order to practise them or enjoy them as a living truth, but, like the rules of a dead language, in order to revere in silence the noble existence of past epochs which have perished for ever.

Since Palladio keeps referring to Vitruvius, I have bought Galliani's edition, but this tome weighs as heavy in my luggage as it weighs on my brain when I study it. I find Palladio, by his own way of thinking and creating, a much better interpreter of Vitruvius than his Italian translator. Vitruvius is not easy reading: the book is written in an obscure style and needs to be studied critically. I skim through the pages or, to be more exact, I read it like a breviary, more from devotion than for instruction.

Already the sun sets earlier and I have more time for reading and writing.

Everything that was important to me in early childhood is again, thank God, becoming dear to me, and, to my joy, I find that I can once again dare to approach the classics. Now, at last, I can confess a secret malady, or mania, of mine. For many years I did not dare look into a Latin author or at anything which evoked an image of Italy. If this happened by chance, I suffered agonies. Herder often used to say mockingly that I had learned all my Latin from Spinoza, for that was the only Latin book he had ever seen me reading. He did not realize how carefully I had to guard myself against the classics, and that it was sheer anxiety which drove me to take refuge in the abstractions of Spinoza. Even quite recently, Wieland's translation of Horace's *Satires* made me very unhappy; after reading only a couple, I felt beside myself.

My passionate desire to see these objects with my own eyes had grown to such a point that, if I had not taken the decision I am now acting upon, I should have gone completely to pieces. More historical knowledge was no help. The things were in arm's reach, yet I felt separated from them by an impenetrable barrier. Now I feel, not that I am seeing them for the first time, but that I am seeing them again.

I arrived here at seven in the morning, German time, and expect to leave again tomorrow. For the first time on my trip, I am in low spirits and feel utterly indifferent to this beautiful, depopulated city in the middle of a flat plain. Once upon a time these same streets were animated by a brilliant court. Here Ariosto lived disappointed and Tasso unhappy, and we persuade ourselves that we are edified by visiting their shrines. The mausoleum of Ariosto contains a great deal of badly distributed marble. Instead of Tasso's prison we are shown a woodshed or coal cellar in which he was certainly not confined. At first nobody in the house knows what one wants to see. After a while they remember, but not before they have been tipped. I was reminded of Dr. Luther's famous ink stain which is touched up from time to time by the custodian of the castle. There must be something of an itinerant journeyman about most travellers to make them want to look for such signs. I got more and more depressed and was only moderately attracted by a beautiful academic institute which a native-born cardinal had founded and endowed. But some monuments of antiquity restored me to life.

I was further cheered up by a painting of John the Baptist confronting Herod and Herodias. The prophet, in his conventional desert costume, is pointing at the lady with a vehement gesture. She looks impassively at the king, sitting beside her, while he looks calmly but shrewdly at the enthusiast. At the feet of the king stands a white dog of medium size, while a small Bolognese dog peeps out from under Herodias' skirt. Both dogs are barking at the prophet. What a jolly idea!

BOLOGNA, OCTOBER 18. NIGHT

I left Cento early this morning and arrived here soon after. As soon as he heard that I had no intention of staying long, an alert, well-informed guide raced me through the streets and so many churches and palaces that I scarcely had time to mark in my Volkmann the places I visited, and who knows, if I look at the marks in the future, how many of them I shall remember. But now for a few highlights.

First of all, the Cecilia by Raphael. My eyes confirmed what I have always known: this man accomplished what others could only dream of. What can one really say about this picture except that Raphael painted it! Five saints in a row—their names don't matter—so perfectly realized that one would be content to die so long as this picture could endure for ever. But, in order to understand and appreciate Raphael properly, one must not merely glorify him as a god who appeared suddenly on earth without a father or a mother, like Melchizedek; one must consider his ancestors, his masters. These were rooted in the firm ground of truth; it was their labour and scrupulous care which laid the broad foundation; it was they who vied with each other in raising, step by step, the pyramid, on the summit of which the divine genius of Raphael was to place the last stone and reach a height which no one else will surpass or equal.

My historical interest has been greatly stimulated by looking at paintings by some of the older masters, such as Francesco Francia, a very fine painter, or Pietro de Perugia, such a good man that one feels like calling him an honest German soul. If only Dürer had had the good fortune to go further south in Italy. Poor Dürer! To think how such a genius—I saw some incredibly great works by him in Munich—miscalculated in Venice and made a deal with a priestly gang which lost him months of his time, and how, when he was travelling in the Netherlands, he bartered the supreme works of art with which he had hoped to make his fortune for parrots, and made portraits of the servants, who had brought him a plate of fruit, to save himself tips! The thought of such a poor fool of an artist is especially moving to me because, at bottom, my fate is the same as his; the only difference is that I know better how to look after myself.

This is a venerable, learned city, thronged with people. They wander about under the arcades which line most of the streets and shelter them from sun and rain as they buy and sell, do business, or stand and gape. Towards evening I escaped from these crowds and climbed the tower to enjoy the fresh air and the view. To the north I could see the hills of Padua, and beyond them the Swiss, Tirolean and Friulian Alps, the whole northern chain, in fact, which at the time was wrapped in mist; in the west, a limitless horizon, broken only by the towers of Modena; to the east, a dead level plain stretching to the Adriatic; and, to the south, the foothills of the Apennines, cultivated right up to their summits and dotted with churches and country houses like the hills of Vicenza.

There was not a cloud in the sky, but on the horizon hung a haze which the watchman of the tower told me had not disappeared for the last six years. The hills of Vicenza with their houses and little churches used to be clearly visible through a telescope, but nowadays this is rare, even on the clearest days. This fog clings by preference to the northern mountain chain and it is this that makes our dear fatherland such a Cimmerian country.

The watchman also pointed out that, thanks to the healthy air, all the roofs of the town looked brand-new; not a tile had been affected by damp or overgrown by moss. This was true, but probably the quality of the tiles has something to do with it. In former times, at least, the tiles baked in this region were of excellent quality.

The leaning tower is frightful to look at, but it was probably built that way on purpose. My theory is that, during the times of civic feuds, every great building became a fortress and every powerful family built its own tower. After a bit, this became both a hobby and a point of honour; everybody wished to boast of having a tower. In due time perpendicular towers became too commonplace, so someone built a leaning one. If so, one must admit that architect and owner achieved their aim, for people are no longer interested in all the straight towers but only in the crooked one. I went up it later. The layers of bricks run horizontally. Given a good mortar and iron bars, it is possible to build the craziest things.

PERUGIA, OCTOBER 25. EVENING

For two evenings I have written nothing. The inns were so bad that I could not find room even to spread out a sheet of paper. Moreover, since leaving Venice, my travelling spool does not reel off as pleasantly and smoothly as it did before, and everything is beginning to get in a muddle.

At ten o'clock our time, on the twenty-third, we emerged from the Apennines and saw Florence lying in a broad valley which was amazingly densely cultivated and scattered with villas and houses as far as the eye could see.

I took a quick walk through the city to see the Duomo and the Battistero. Once more, a completely new world opened up before me, but I did not wish to stay long. The location of the Boboli Gardens is marvellous. I hurried out of the city as quickly as I entered it.

One look is sufficient to show one that the people who built it were prosperous and enjoyed a lucky succession of good governments. The most striking thing about Tuscany is that all the public works, the roads and the bridges, look beautiful and imposing. They are at one and the same time efficient and neat, combining usefulness with grace, and everywhere one observes the care with which things are looked after, a refreshing contrast to the Papal States, which seem to keep alive only because the earth refuses to swallow them.

All that I recently said the Apennines might have been, Tuscany is, for it lies so much lower, the ancient sea has done its duty and piled up a deep loamy soil. This is light yellow in colour and easy to work. The peasants plough deep furrows but still in the old-fashioned manner. Their plough has no wheels and the share is not movable. Hunched behind his oxen, the peasant pushes his plough into the earth to break it up. They plough up to five times a year and use only a little light manure which they scatter with their hands. At sowing time, they heap up small, narrow ridges with deep furrows between them in which the rain water can run off. The wheat grows on the top of the ridges, so that they can walk up and down the furrows when they weed. In a region where there is a danger of too much rain, this method would be very sensible, but why they do it in this wonderful climate, I cannot understand. I saw them doing this near Arezzo. It would be difficult to find cleaner fields anywhere; one cannot see the smallest clod of earth; the soil is as clean as if it had been sifted. Wheat seems to find here all the conditions most favourable to its growth, and does very well. Every second year, they grow beans for the horses, which are not fed on oats. The lupines are already green and will be ripe in March. The flax is coming up. It is left out all winter and the frost only makes it all the more hardy.

Olives are strange trees; they look almost like willows, for they too lose their heartwood and their bark splits open, but they look sturdier. The wood grows slowly, and is very fine-grained. The leaf is similar to a willow leaf, but there are fewer to a branch. Around Florence, all the hill slopes are planted with olives and vines, and the soil between them is used for grain. Near Arezzo and further on, the fields are less cluttered. In my opinion, they do not check the ivy enough; it does great damage to the olives and other trees, and it would be easy to destroy. There are no meadows anywhere. I was told that maize had exhausted the soil. Since it was introduced, agriculture has declined in other ways. I believe this comes from using so little manure.

FOLIGNO, OCTOBER 26. EVENING

I left Perugia on a glorious morning and felt the bliss of being once more alone. The situation of the town is beautiful and the view of the lake charming. I shall remember them both. At first the road went downhill, then it ran along a lovely valley, flanked on either side by distant hills, until, finally, Assisi came into view.

From reading Palladio and Volkmann, I knew there was a Temple of Minerva here, built during the reign of Augustus and still perfectly preserved. When we got near

Madonna degli Angeli, I left my *vetturino* and let him go on to Foligno. I was longing to take a walk by myself in this silent world, and climbed the road to Assisi on foot with a high wind blowing against me. I turned away in distaste from the enormous substructure of the two churches on my left, which are built one on top of the other like a Babylonian tower, and are the resting place of St. Francis. I was afraid that the people who gathered there would be of the same stamp as my captain. I asked a handsome boy the way to the Maria della Minerva, and he accompanied me up into the town, which is built on the side of a hill. At last we arrived in the Old Town and—lo and behold!—there it stood, the first complete classical monument I have seen. A modest temple, just right for such a small town, yet so perfect in design that it would be an ornament anywhere.

Since I have read in Vitruvius and Palladio how cities should be laid out and how temples and public buildings should be situated, I have learned to treat these matters with great respect. In this, as in so much else, the ancients were great by instinct. The temple is situated halfway up the mountain at a point where two hills meet and on a piece of level ground which today is called the *piazza*. The square itself slopes slightly and four roads meet there, two from above and two from below, forming an irregular St. Andrew's Cross. In ancient times the houses which face the temple and obstruct the view probably did not exist. If they were removed, one could look down on the fertile countryside to the south and the sanctuary of Minerva would be visible from every side. The layout of the roads may be of early date, since they follow the contours of the mountain. The temple does not stand in the centre of the square but is so placed that it can be seen in foreshortened perspective by anyone approaching it from the direction of Rome. Besides drawing the building, one ought to draw its well-chosen site.

One could never tire of looking at the façade and admiring the logical procedure of the architect. The order is Corinthian and the space between the columns about two modules. The bases of the columns and the plinths below them appear to be standing on pedestals, but this is only an illusion, for the stylobate has been cut through in five places, and through each gap five steps lead up between the columns. By these one reaches the platform on which the columns actually stand, and enters the temple. The bold idea of cutting through the stylobate was a very sensible one, given the site. Since the temple stands on a hill, the stairs up to it would otherwise have jutted out too far into the square and made it too cramped. How many steps there were originally is now impossible to determine, because, except for a few, they lie buried under the earth and paved over. I tore myself away reluctantly and firmly resolved to call the attention of all architects to this building so that an accurate plan may be made available to us. I realized once more how little accepted tradition is to be trusted. Palladio, on whom I had relied implicitly, made a sketch of this temple, but he cannot have seen it personally, for he puts real pedestals on the ground, which gives the columns a disproportionate height and makes the whole a Palmyra-like monstrosity instead of the great loveliness of the real thing. I cannot describe the sensations which this work aroused in me, but I know they are going to bear fruit for ever.

The evening was beautiful and I was walking down the Roman Road in a state of blissful content when suddenly behind me I heard loud, rough voices in lively argument. I thought they must be *sbirri*, for I had previously noticed some in the town. Without turning round, but straining my ears to catch what they were saying, I walked calmly on. Soon I realized that I was the subject of their quarrel. Four men, two of them armed with guns, passed me, muttering something. After a few steps they turned, surrounded me, and asked what I was doing here. I replied that I was a stranger and had walked to Assisi while my *vetturino* drove on to Foligno. This they found hard to believe—that someone should pay for a carriage and then walk. They asked if I had been to the Gran Convento. I said no, but assured them I had known the building for many years. This time, since I was an architect, I had gone to look at the Maria della Minerva, which, as they knew, was an architectural masterpiece. This they did not deny, but they were offended because I had not paid my respects to the saint and did not conceal their suspicion that I might be a dealer in contraband goods. I pointed out how ridiculous it was to take someone for a smuggler who was walking by himself without a knapsack and with empty pockets. I offered to return to the town with them and go to the *podestà*. I would show him my documents and he would acknowledge me as a respectable foreigner. After muttering among themselves again, they said this would be unnecessary. I behaved all the time with dignity and, at last, they went away towards the town. I followed them with my eye. There, in the foreground, walked those rude fellows while, behind them, Minerva looked down on me kindly, as if she wanted to console me. I turned to look at the dreary Duomo of St. Francis on my left and was just about to continue my way when one of the unarmed members of the band left it and approached me in a friendly manner. "Dear Mr. Foreigner," he said, "you ought, at least, to give me a tip, for, I assure you, I knew at once that you were an honest man and frankly told my companions so. But they are hot-headed, quick-tempered fellows who do not know the ways of the world. You must also have noticed that I was the first to applaud your words and back you up." I complimented him on this and urged him to protect in future any distinguished foreigner who might come to Assisi for the sake of religion and art, especially any architect who might come to measure and sketch the Temple of Minerva, which had never yet been drawn or engraved. Such people would bring glory to the town, and if he gave them a helping hand, they would certainly show their gratitude—and with these words I pressed a few silver coins into his hand, which made him very happy, as they were more than he had expected. He begged me to come back to Assisi soon; I must on no account miss the feast of the saint, when I could certainly expect both edification and amusement. Indeed, if a good-looking man like me should wish to meet a handsome female, he could assure me that, on his recommendation, the most beautiful and respectable woman in Assisi would gladly receive me. He then took his leave, after solemnly promising that he would remember me that very evening in his devotions at the tomb of the saint and pray for the success of my journey. So we parted, and I felt much relieved at being alone again with

Nature and myself. The road to Foligno along the side of the mountain overlooking the valley is beautiful, and my walk, which took fully four hours, was one of the most enchanting I have ever taken.

Travelling with *vetturini* is an exhausting affair; the only thing to be said for it is that one can always get out and walk. All the way from Ferrara I have submitted to being dragged along in this fashion. This Italy, so greatly favoured by Nature, has lagged far behind all other countries in mechanical and technical matters, which are, after all, the basis of a comfortable, agreeable life. The carriage of the *vetturino* is called *una sedia,* "a seat", and is undoubtedly derived from the ancient litters in which women and elderly or prominent persons were carried by mules. The mule that was harnessed between the shafts of the rear has been replaced by two wheels, and that is all the improvement they have made. One is still joggled along as one was centuries ago. It is the same with their houses and everything else. The idyllic dream of the first men living out of doors and retiring to caves only in an emergency is a reality here, and to see it, one has only to enter their dwellings, especially in rural districts, which still preserve the character of caves.

They are utterly carefree because they are afraid that thinking might make them age quicker. With an unheard-of negligence they fail to make provision for the longer winter nights and, consequently, suffer like dogs for a considerable part of the year. The inn here in Foligno is exactly like a Homeric household. Everyone is gathered in a large vault around an open fireplace, shouting and talking. They all eat together at one long table, as in a painting of the Wedding Feast at Cana. To my great surprise, someone has brought me an inkwell, so I am taking the opportunity to write, though these pages will bear witness to the cold and the inconvenience of my writing table.

I have only just realized how bold I was to travel unprepared and alone through this country. The different currencies, the *vetturini*, the prices, the wretched inns are a daily nuisance, and anyone who travels alone for the first time, hoping for uninterrupted pleasures, is bound to be often disappointed and have much to put up with. But, after all, my one wish has been to see this country at any cost and, were I to be dragged to Rome on Ixion's wheel, I should not utter a single word of complaint.

At last I can break my silence and send my friends a joyful greeting. I hope they will forgive me for my secretiveness and my almost subterranean journey to this country. Even to myself, I hardly dared admit where I was going and all the way I was still afraid I might be dreaming; it was not till I had passed through the Porta-del Popolo that I was certain it was true, that I really was in Rome.

Let me also say this: here in Rome, in the presence of all those objects which I never expected to see by myself, you are constantly in my thoughts. It was only when I realized that everyone at home was chained, body and soul, to the north, and all desire to visit these parts had vanished, that, drawn by an irresistable need, I made up my mind to undertake this long, solitary journey to the hub of the world.

Now that this need has been satisfied, my friends and my native land have once again become very dear to my heart, and my desire to return very keen, all the keener because I am convinced that the many treasures I shall bring home with me will serve both myself and others as a guide and an education for a lifetime.

Now, at last, I have arrived in the First City of the world! Had I seen it fifteen years ago with an intelligent man to guide me, I should have called myself lucky, but, since I was destined to visit it alone and trust to my own eyes, I am happy, at least, to have been granted this joy so late in life.

Across the mountains of the Tirol I fled rather than travelled. Vicenza, Padua and Venice I saw thoroughly, Ferrara, Cento, Bologna casually, and Florence hardly at all. My desire to reach Rome quickly was growing stronger every minute until nothing could have induced me to make more stops, so that I spent only three hours there. Now I have arrived, I have calmed down and feel as if I had found a peace that will last for my whole life. Because, if I may say so, as soon as one sees with one's own eyes the whole which one had hitherto only known in fragments and chaotically, a new life begins.

All the dreams of my youth have come to life; the first engravings I remember—my father hung views of Rome in the hall—I now see in reality, and everything I have known for so long through paintings, drawings, etchings, woodcuts, plaster casts and cork models is now assembled before me. Wherever I walk, I come upon familiar objects in an unfamiliar world; everything is just as I imagined it, yet everything is new. It is the same with my observations and ideas. I have not had a single idea which was entirely new or surprising, but my old ideas have become so much more firm, vital and coherent that they could be called new.

When Pygmalion's Galatea, whom he had fashioned exactly after his dreams, endowing her with as much reality and existence as an artist can, finally came up to him and said: "Here I am," how different was the living woman from the sculptured stone.

Besides, for me it is morally salutary to be living in the midst of a sensual people about whom so much has been said and written, and whom every foreigner judges by the standard he brings with him. I can excuse those who criticize and disapprove of them because their life is so far removed from ours, that it is difficult and expensive for a foreigner to have dealings with them.

NOVEMBER 5

I have been here now for seven days and am gradually beginning to get a general idea of the city. We walk about a good deal, I study the layout of Ancient Rome and Modern Rome, look at ruins and buildings and visit this villa or that. The most important monuments I take very slowly; I do nothing except look, go away, and come back and look again. Only in Rome can one educate oneself for Rome.

I find it a difficult and melancholy business, I must confess, separating the old Rome from the new, but it has to be done and I can only hope that, in the end, my efforts will prove well worth while. One comes upon traces both of magnificence and of devastation, which stagger the imagination. What the barbarians left, the builders of Modern Rome have destroyed.

Here is an entity which has suffered so many drastic changes in the course of two thousand years, yet is still the same soil, the same hill, often even the same column or the same wall, and in its people one still finds traces of their ancient character. Contemplating this, the observer becomes, at it were, a contemporary of the great decrees of destiny, and this makes it difficult for him to follow the evolution of the city, to grasp not only how Modern Rome follows on Ancient, but also how, within both, one epoch follows upon another. I shall first of all try to grope my way along this half-hidden track by myself, for only after I have done that shall I be able to benefit from the excellent preliminary studies to which, from the fifteenth century till today, eminent scholars and artists have devoted their lives.

As I rush about Rome looking at the major monuments, the immensity of the place has a quietening effect. In other places one has to search for the important points of interest; here they crowd in on one in profusion. Wherever you turn your eyes, every kind of vista, near and distant, confronts you—palaces, ruins, gardens, wildernesses, small houses, stables, triumphal arches, columns—all of them often so close together that they could be sketched on a single sheet of paper. One would need a thousand styluses to write with. What can one do here with a single pen? And then, in the evening, one feels exhausted after so much looking and admiring.

NOVEMBER 9

Sometimes I stand still for a moment and survey, as it were, the high peaks of my experiences so far. I look back with special joy to Venice, that great being who sprang from the sea like Pallas from the head of Jupiter. In Rome the Pantheon, so great within and without, has overwhelmed me with admiration. St. Peter's has made me realize that Art, like Nature, can abolish all standards of measurement. The Apollo Belvedere has also swept me off my feet. Just as the most accurate drawings fail to give an adequate idea of these buildings, so plaster casts, good as some I have seen are, can be no substitute for their marble originals.

NOVEMBER 10

I am now in a state of clarity and calm such as I had not known for a long time. My habit of looking at and accepting things as they are without pretension is standing me in good stead and makes me secretly very happy. Each day brings me some new remarkable object, some new great picture, and a whole city which the imagination will never encompass, however long one thinks and dreams.

Today I went to the pyramid of Cestius and in the evening climbed to the top of the Palatine, where the ruins of the imperial palaces stand like rocks. It is impossible to convey a proper idea of such things. Nothing here is mediocre, and if, here and there, something is in poor taste, it, too, shares in the general grandeur.

When I indulge in self-reflection, as I like to do occasionally, I discover in myself a feeling which gives me great joy. Let me put it like this. In this place, whoever looks seriously about him and has eyes to see is bound to become a stronger character: he acquires a sense of strength hitherto unknown to him.

His soul receives the seal of a soundness, a seriousness without pedantry, and a joyous composure. At least, I can say that I have never been so sensitive to the things of this world as I am here. The blessed consequences will, I believe, affect my whole future life.

So let me seize things one by one as they come; they will sort themselves out later. I am not here simply to have a good time, but to devote myself to the noble objects about me, to educate myself before I reach forty.

NOVEMBER 11

Today I visited the Nymph Egeria, the Circus of Caracalla, the ruined tombs along the Via Appia and the tomb of Metella, which made me realize for the first time what solid masonry means. These people built for eternity; they omitted nothing from their calculations except the insane fury of the destroyers to whom nothing was sacred.

I also saw the ruins of the great aqueduct. What a noble ambition it showed, to raise a tremendous construction for the sake of supplying water to a people. We came to

the Colosseum at twilight. Once one has seen it, everything else seems small. It is so huge that the mind cannot
retain its image; one remembers it as smaller than it is, so
that every time one returns to it, one is again astounded
by its size.

NOVEMBER 22

ON THE FEAST OF ST. CECILIA

I must write a few lines to keep alive the memory of this
happy day or, at least, make a historical report of what I
have been enjoying. The day was cloudless and warm. I
went with Tischbein to the square in front of St. Peter's.
We walked up and down until we felt too hot, when we
sat in the shadow of the great obelisk—it was just wide
enough for two—and ate some grapes we had bought
nearby. Then we went into the Sistine Chapel, where the
light on the frescoes was at its best. Looking at these marvellous works of Michelangelo's, our admiration was
divided between the Last Judgment and the various
paintings on the ceiling. The self-assurance, the virility,
the grandeur of conception of this master defy expression. After we had looked at everything over and over
again, we left the chapel and entered St. Peter's. Thanks to

82

the brilliant sunshine outside, every part of the church was visible. Since we were determined to enjoy its magnitude and splendour, we did not, this time, allow our over-fastidious taste to put us off and abstained from carping criticism. We enjoyed everything that was enjoyable.

Then we climbed up on the roof, where one finds a miniature copy of a well-built town with houses, shops, fountains, churches (at least they looked like churches from the outside) and a large temple—everything in the open air with beautiful walks between. We went into the Cupola and looked out at the Apennines, Mount Soracte, the volcanic hills behind Tivoli, Frascati, Castel Gandolfo, the plain and the sea beyond it. Below us lay the city of Rome in all its length and breadth with its hill-perched palaces, domes, etc. Not a breath of air was stirring, and it was as hot as a greenhouse inside the copper ball. After taking in everything, we descended again and asked to have the doors opened which lead to the cornices of the dome, the tambour and the nave. One can walk all the way round and look down from this height on the whole church. As we were standing on the cornice of the tambour, far below us we could see the Pope walking to make his afternoon devotions. St. Peter's had not failed us. Then we climbed all the way down, went out into the square and had a frugal but cheerful meal at an inn nearby, after which we went on to the Church of St. Cecilia.

It would take pages to describe the decorations of this church, which was packed with people. One could not see a stone of the structure. The columns were covered with red velvet wound around with ribbons of gold lace, the capitals with embroidered velvet conforming more or less to their shape—so, too, with the cornices and pillars. All the intervening wall space was clothed in brightly coloured hangings, so that the whole church seemed to be one enormous mosaic. More than two hundred candles were burning behind and at the sides of the high altar, so that one whole wall was lined with candles, and the nave was fully illuminated. Facing the high altar, two stands, also covered with velvet, had been erected under the organ loft. The singers stood on one; the orchestra, which never stopped playing, on the other.

Just as there are concertos for violins or other instruments, here they perform concertos for voices: one voice—the soprano, for instance—predominates and sings a solo while, from time to time, the choir joins in and accompanies it, always supported, of course, by the full orchestra. The effect is wonderful.

All good days must come to an end and so must these notes. In the evening we got to the opera house, where *i Litiganti* was being given, but we were so sated with good things that we passed it by.

DECEMBER 2

By chance, I came across Archenholz's book on Italy. When one reads it here, it is incredible how such a scribble shrinks to nothing. It's as if one had thrown it in the fire, and watched it slowly turn brown and black, till the pages curled and went up in smoke. The author has seen everything, of course; but he knows far too little to excuse his overbearing, contemptuous tone, and, whether he is praising or blaming, he makes blunders all the time.

To have beautiful warm weather, with only an occasional rainy day, at the end of November is a new experience for me. We spend the fine days out of doors, the wet ones in our room, and always find something to enjoy, to study or to do.

On November 28 we visited the Sistine Chapel again and got them to open the gallery for us, because from there the ceiling can be seen at closer range. The gallery is rather narrow and we squeezed into it along the iron railing with some difficulty and some feeling of danger—people who suffer from vertigo would be advised to stay below—but this was more than made up for by the masterpiece which met our eyes. At present I am so enthusiastic about Michelangelo that I have lost all my taste for Nature, since I cannot see her with the eye of genius as he did. If only there were some means of fixing such images firmly in one's memory! At any rate, I shall bring home as many engravings and drawings made after his work as I can get hold of. From the chapel we went to the loggias of Raphael, and, though I hardly dare admit it, I could not look at them any longer. After being dilated and spoiled by Michelangelo's great forms, my eye took no pleasure in the ingenious frivolities of Raphael's arabesques, and his Biblical stories, beautiful as they are, do not stand up against Michelangelo's. What a joy it would give me if I could see the works of both more frequently and compare them at leisure without prejudice, for one's initial reactions are bound to be one-sided.

The sun was almost too warm as we dragged ourselves to the Villa Pamfili and stayed in its lovely gardens until evening. A large meadow, bordered with evergreen oaks and tall stone-pines, was dotted with daisies which all had their little heads turned to the sun. This set me off again on botanical speculations, which I resumed the next day during a walk to Monte Mario, Villa Mellini and Villa Madama. It is fascinating to observe how a vegetation behaves when its lively growth is never interrupted by severe cold. One sees no buds here and realizes for the first time what a bud is. The arbutus is again in bloom while its last fruits are still ripening. The orange trees also show blossoms, as well as half- and fully-ripe fruits, but these, unless they stand between buildings, are covered at this time of year. There is room for speculation about the cypress, which, when it is very old and full-grown, is the most dignified of all trees. Soon I shall pay a visit to the Botanical Garden, where I hope to learn a good deal. Nothing, above all, is comparable to the new life that a reflective person experiences when he observes a new country. Though I am still always myself, I believe I have been changed to the very marrow of my bones.

DECEMBER 3

Till now the weather has followed a six-day cycle—two cloudless days, one overcast day, two or three wet days and then again fine weather. I try to make the best use I can of each one of them.

The noble objects with which I am surrounded never lose their freshness for me. I did not grow up with them. I have not wrung from each its peculiar secret. Some attract me so powerfully that, for a while, I become indifferent, even unjust, to others. For example, the Pantheon, the Apollo Belvedere, one or two colossal heads and, recently, the Sistine Chapel have so obsessed me that I see almost nothing else. But how can we, petty as we are and accustomed to pettiness, ever become equal to such noble perfection? Even when one has adjusted oneself to some degree, a tremendous mass of new things crowd in on one, facing one at every step, each demanding the tribute of one's attention. How is one to find one's way through? Only by patiently allowing it all to grow slowly inside one, and by industriously studying what others have written for one's benefit.

I immediately bought the new edition of Winckelmann's *History of the Art of Antiquity*, translated by Fea. Read on the spot where it was written and with an able and learned company to consult, I find it a great help.

Roman antiquity is beginning to give me about as much pleasure as Greek. History, inscriptions, coins, in which hitherto I took no interest, are forcing themselves on my attention. My experience with natural history is repeating itself here, for the entire history of the world is linked up with this city, and I reckon my second life, a very rebirth, from the day when I entered Rome.

I am so happy that you have taken my disappearance as well as I hoped you would. Please make my peace with any heart that may have been offended at it. I did not mean to upset anyone and I cannot yet say anything to justify myself. God forbid that the motives which led to my decision should ever hurt the feelings of a friend.

I am slowly recovering from my *"salto mortale"*, and I study more than I amuse myself. Rome is a world, and it would take years to become a true citizen of it. How lucky those travellers are who take one look and leave.

This morning I came by chance on the letters which Winckelmann wrote from Italy, and you can imagine with what emotion I have started to read them. Thirty-one years ago, at the same time of year, he arrived here, an even greater fool than I was. But, with true German seriousness, he set himself to make a thorough and accurate study of antiquity and its arts. How bravely he worked his way through! And, in this city, what it means to me to remember him!

Aside from the objects of Nature, who in all her realms is true and consistent, nothing speaks so loudly as the impression left by a good and intelligent man, or by authentic works of art which are just as unerring as Nature. One feels this particularly strongly in Rome, where so many caprices have been given free rein and so many absurdities perpetuated by wealth and power.

I was especially delighted by one passage in a letter of Winckelmann's to Francke. "In Rome you must seek out everything with a certain phlegm, otherwise you are taken for a Frenchman. I believe that Rome is the school for the whole world and I, too, have been purged and tested here."

What he says exactly describes my methods of investigation. No one who has not been here can have any conception of what an education Rome is. One is, so to speak, reborn and one's former ideas seem like a child's swaddling clothes. Here the most ordinary person becomes somebody, for his mind is enormously enlarged even if his character remains unchanged.

This letter will reach you in time for the New Year. May its beginning bring you much happiness and may we all meet again before its end! What a joy that will be! The past year has been the most important in my life; whether I die tomorrow or live yet awhile, it has been good to me.

PENGUIN 60s CLASSICS

APOLLONIUS OF RHODES · *Jason and the Argonauts*
ARISTOPHANES · *Lysistrata*
SAINT AUGUSTINE · *Confessions of a Sinner*
JANE AUSTEN · *The History of England*
HONORÉ DE BALZAC · *The Atheist's Mass*
BASHŌ · *Haiku*
GIOVANNI BOCCACCIO · *Ten Tales from the Decameron*
JAMES BOSWELL · *Meeting Dr Johnson*
CHARLOTTE BRONTË · *Mina Laury*
CAO XUEQIN · *The Dream of the Red Chamber*
THOMAS CARLYLE · *On Great Men*
BALDESAR CASTIGLIONE · *Etiquette for Renaissance Gentlemen*
CERVANTES · *The Jealous Extremaduran*
KATE CHOPIN · *The Kiss*
JOSEPH CONRAD · *The Secret Sharer*
DANTE · *The First Three Circles of Hell*
CHARLES DARWIN · *The Galapagos Islands*
THOMAS DE QUINCEY · *The Pleasures and Pains of Opium*
DANIEL DEFOE · *A Visitation of the Plague*
BERNAL DÍAZ · *The Betrayal of Montezuma*
FYODOR DOSTOYEVSKY · *The Gentle Spirit*
FREDERICK DOUGLASS · *The Education of Frederick Douglass*
GEORGE ELIOT · *The Lifted Veil*
GUSTAVE FLAUBERT · *A Simple Heart*
BENJAMIN FRANKLIN · *The Means and Manner of Obtaining Virtue*
EDWARD GIBBON · *Reflections on the Fall of Rome*
CHARLOTTE PERKINS GILMAN · *The Yellow Wallpaper*
GOETHE · *Letters from Italy*
HOMER · *The Rage of Achilles*
HOMER · *The Voyages of Odysseus*

PENGUIN 60s CLASSICS

HENRY JAMES · *The Lesson of the Master*
FRANZ KAFKA · *The Judgement*
THOMAS À KEMPIS · *Counsels on the Spiritual Life*
HEINRICH VON KLEIST · *The Marquise of O—*
LIVY · *Hannibal's Crossing of the Alps*
NICCOLÒ MACHIAVELLI · *The Art of War*
SIR THOMAS MALORY · *The Death of King Arthur*
GUY DE MAUPASSANT · *Boule de Suif*
FRIEDRICH NIETZSCHE · *Zarathustra's Discourses*
OVID · *Orpheus in the Underworld*
PLATO · *Phaedrus*
EDGAR ALLAN POE · *The Murders in the Rue Morgue*
ARTHUR RIMBAUD · *A Season in Hell*
JEAN-JACQUES ROUSSEAU · *Meditations of a Solitary Walker*
ROBERT LOUIS STEVENSON · *Dr Jekyll and Mr Hyde*
TACITUS · *Nero and the Burning of Rome*
HENRY DAVID THOREAU · *Civil Disobedience*
LEO TOLSTOY · *The Death of Ivan Ilyich*
IVAN TURGENEV · *Three Sketches from a Hunter's Album*
MARK TWAIN · *The Man That Corrupted Hadleyburg*
GIORGIO VASARI · *Lives of Three Renaissance Artists*
EDITH WHARTON · *Souls Belated*
WALT WHITMAN · *Song of Myself*
OSCAR WILDE · *The Portrait of Mr W. H.*

ANONYMOUS WORKS

Beowulf and Grendel   *Buddha's Teachings*
Gilgamesh and Enkidu   *Krishna's Dialogue on the Soul*
Tales of Cú Chulaind   *Two Viking Romances*

READ MORE IN PENGUIN

For complete information about books available from Penguin and how to order them, please write to us at the appropriate address below. Please note that for copyright reasons the selection of books varies from country to country.

IN THE UNITED KINGDOM: Please write to *Dept. JC, Penguin Books Ltd, FREEPOST, West Drayton, Middlesex UB7 0BR.*
If you have any difficulty in obtaining a title, please send your order with the correct money, plus ten per cent for postage and packaging, to *PO Box No. 11, West Drayton, Middlesex UB7 0BR.'*

IN THE UNITED STATES: Please write to *Consumer Sales, Penguin USA, P.O. Box 999, Dept. 17109, Bergenfield, New Jersey 07621-0120.* VISA and MasterCard holders call 1-800-253-6476 to order all Penguin titles.

IN CANADA: Please write to *Penguin Books Canada Ltd, 10 Alcorn Avenue, Suite 300, Toronto, Ontario M4V 3B2.*

IN AUSTRALIA: Please write to *Penguin Books Australia Ltd, P.O. Box 257, Ringwood, Victoria 3134.*

IN NEW ZEALAND: Please write to *Penguin Books (NZ) Ltd, Private Bag 102902, North Shore Mail Centre, Auckland 10.*

IN INDIA: Please write to *Penguin Books India Pvt Ltd, 706 Eros Apartments, 56 Nehru Place, New Delhi 110 019.*

IN THE NETHERLANDS: Please write to *Penguin Books Netherlands bv, Postbus 3507, NL-1001 AH Amsterdam.*

IN GERMANY: Please write to *Penguin Books Deutschland GmbH, Metzlerstrasse 26, 60594 Frankfurt am Main.*

IN SPAIN: Please write to *Penguin Books S. A., Bravo Murillo 19, 1° B, 28015 Madrid.*

IN ITALY: Please write to *Penguin Italia s.r.l., Via Felice Casati 20, I–20124 Milano.*

IN FRANCE: Please write to *Penguin France S. A., 17 rue Lejeune, F–31000 Toulouse.*

IN JAPAN: Please write to *Penguin Books Japan, Ishikiribashi Building, 2-5-4, Suido, Bunkyo-ku, Tokyo 112.*

IN GREECE: Please write to *Penguin Hellas Ltd, Dimocritou 3, GR–106 71 Athens.*

IN SOUTH AFRICA: Please write to *Longman Penguin Southern Africa (Pty) Ltd, Private Bag X08, Bertsham 2013.*